# Guide to SQLite

Practical Guide

A. De Quattro

Copyright © 2024

# Guide to SQLite

# 1.Introduction

SQLite is a lightweight, in-process, self-contained relational database management system (DBMS). This means that SQLite is a software library that provides a complete and standalone SQL database without the need for a separate server. SQLite is widely used as an embedded database in desktop, mobile, and web software applications, as it is lightweight, fast, and offers a wide range of standard relational database features.

SQLite was created by Dwayne Richard Hipp in 2000 and released as open-source software, making it freely available to all developers. Being a C library written in the C language, SQLite is highly portable and can be used on a wide range of platforms, including desktop operating systems like Windows, macOS, and Linux, as well as mobile platforms like Android and iOS.

One of the distinctive features of SQLite is its

support for ACID transactions (Atomicity, Consistency, Isolation, Durability), which ensures that database changes are always secure, consistent, and durable. This makes it suitable for applications where data integrity is essential, such as financial applications, inventory management systems, and more.

In SQLite, data is stored in single database files that can be easily transferred, shared, and copied without the need to set up a separate server. Additionally, SQLite supports a wide range of data types, including text, numbers, dates, images, and binary blobs, offering versatility in data management.

SQLite comes with a complete SQL interface that allows developers to intuitively and flexibly create, read, update, and delete data. Developers can use standard SQL statements to query the database, create tables, define constraints, and manage indexes to optimize query performance.

SQLite also offers a wide range of advanced features, such as the ability to create triggers and stored procedures to automate complex tasks, as well as transaction management and foreign key constraints to ensure data referential integrity.

Furthermore, SQLite supports data indexing to improve query performance and offers the ability to use aggregation functions and window functions to process data in complex and advanced ways.

Lastly, SQLite is highly scalable and can easily handle large databases with millions of rows of data. Thanks to its lightweight, in-process architecture, SQLite can quickly handle read and write operations, making it ideal for applications that require high concurrency and performance.

SQLite is a powerful, flexible, and versatile database management system that provides a solid foundation for the development of software applications in a wide range of industries and platforms. Its ease of use, robustness, and excellent performance make it a popular choice among developers worldwide.

## 2. Installing SQLite

SQLite is an open-source, lightweight database that offers a self-contained implementation of SQL. It is ideal for small projects or developers who need a local database for their applications. In this guide, I will explain step by step how to install SQLite on your computer and start using it.

Step 1: Download the installation file

The first step to install SQLite is to download the installation file from the official website. You can find it at https://www.sqlite.org/download.html. Make sure to choose the correct version for your operating system (Windows, Linux, MacOS).

Step 2: Extract the installation file

Once you have downloaded the installation file, extract it to the destination folder on your computer. You can do this using compression software like WinRAR or 7-Zip. Make sure to select the correct folder where you want to install SQLite.

## Step 3: Add SQLite to the system PATH (optional)

To make it easier to access SQLite from any directory on your computer, you can add the path where you extracted the installation file to the system PATH environment variable. In Windows, you can do this by going to System Settings -> Environment Variables -> Edit System Environment Variables and adding the path of SQLite to the PATH variable.

## Step 4: Verify the installation

To verify that the SQLite installation was successful, open the command prompt and type "sqlite3". If the installation was successful, you should see an interactive SQLite prompt that allows you to start using the database.

## Step 5: Start using SQLite

Now that SQLite is installed on your computer, you can start creating and managing databases using the interactive prompt or a graphical interface like DB Browser for SQLite. You can create a new database by typing the command "sqlite3 database_name.db" and start using it to create tables, insert data, and run SQL queries.

## Step 6: Use SQLite with a programming language

SQLite is compatible with numerous programming languages such as Python, Java, C#, etc. To use SQLite within an application, make sure to include the correct driver for the language you are using and follow specific instructions for connecting to the database and running queries.

## Step 7: Keep SQLite updated

To ensure optimal and secure functionality of SQLite, make sure to always keep the software version updated. Check the official website periodically for any updates and download them to ensure compatibility with the latest versions of operating systems and libraries.

Now that you have completed the SQLite installation guide, you are ready to start using this lightweight and versatile database for your projects.

## 3. Creating and Managing SQLite Tables

SQLite is a very popular relational database that, unlike other database management systems, does not require a dedicated server to operate. This makes it a very practical choice for applications that require a lightweight and easy-to-use database. One of the main features of SQLite is the creation and management of tables, which are the fundamental element on which to base your database.

To create a table in SQLite, you need to use the SQL query language. First of all, you need to open the database using the `sqlite3` command. Once the database is open, you can create a new table using the `CREATE TABLE` command. For example, if we wanted to create a table called `users` with three columns (id, name, and email), the SQL command would be as follows:

```sql
CREATE TABLE users (
  id INTEGER PRIMARY KEY,
  name TEXT,
```

    email TEXT
);
```

In this example, we are defining a table called `users` with three columns: `id`, `name`, and `email`. The `id` column is defined as a primary key using the data type `INTEGER` and the `PRIMARY KEY` modifier. This means that each row in the table must have a unique value for the `id` column. The `name` and `email` columns are both of type `TEXT`.

Once the table has been created, you can add rows using the `INSERT INTO` command. For example, if we wanted to add a new user with the name `John Doe` and email `john.doe@example.com`, the SQL command would be as follows:

```sql
INSERT INTO users (name, email)
VALUES ('John Doe', 'john.doe@example.com');
```

In this case, we are inserting a new row in the
```

`users` table with the values `John Doe` for the `name` column and `john.doe@example.com` for the `email` column. If we wanted to view all the users in the table, we could use the `SELECT * FROM users` command.

Once the table has been populated with the necessary data, you can modify the data using the `UPDATE` command. For example, if we wanted to change the email of a specific user, the SQL command would be as follows:

```sql
UPDATE users
SET email = 'new.email@example.com'
WHERE name = 'John Doe';
```

In this example, we are updating the `email` column for the user with the name `John Doe` and setting the new value to `new.email@example.com`. You can also delete rows from the table using the `DELETE` command. For example, if we wanted to delete the user with the name `John Doe`, the SQL command would be as follows:

```sql
DELETE FROM users
WHERE name = 'John Doe';
```

Furthermore, you can use the `DROP TABLE` command to completely delete the table and all of its data. For example, if we wanted to delete the `users` table, the SQL command would be as follows:

```sql
DROP TABLE users;
```

Creating and managing tables in SQLite is very simple and intuitive thanks to the SQL query language. It is important to carefully plan the structure of the tables in order to make data access as efficient as possible. Additionally, it is important to maintain data consistency and ensure that all insert, update, and delete operations are carried out correctly. SQLite offers a wide range of features for managing tables, allowing you to create robust and high-performance databases for applications.

# 4. Creating a Table

Before delving into the details of individual fields, it is important to understand the basic concepts regarding defining a table in SQLite. Each table consists of rows and columns, and each column represents a field, which can contain data of different types. For each field, a data type must be specified, which determines the type of data that can be stored in that field and the operations that can be performed on them.

The data types supported by SQLite can be divided into different groups, including:

- Numeric: including INTEGER, REAL, and NUMERIC;
- Textual: TEXT and VARCHAR;
- Date/time: DATE, TIME, and TIMESTAMP.

Each data type has specific characteristics and limitations that should be considered when defining the structure of a table. For example, fields of type INTEGER can contain integer numerical values, while those of type TEXT can contain variable-length text strings.

In addition to the data type, additional options can be specified for the fields, which determine how the data is handled and the validity rules that must be followed. Some of the most common options include:

- PRIMARY KEY: indicates that the field is a primary key, which must be unique for each row in the table and is used to uniquely identify each row;
- AUTOINCREMENT: indicates that the value of the field is automatically generated incrementally for each new row inserted into the table;
- NOT NULL: indicates that the field cannot be NULL and must contain a valid value;
- UNIQUE: indicates that the field must contain unique values for all rows in the table;
- DEFAULT: specifies a default value assigned to the field if a value is not specified during data insertion.

By using these options, the fields of a table can be defined flexibly and tailored to the specific needs of the application. For example, if you want to create a table of users where the user ID must be unique and incremental, you can define the ID field with the INTEGER type and the PRIMARY KEY and AUTOINCREMENT options.

To further illustrate how to define the fields of a table in SQLite, consider a practical example of a "Products" table containing information about a store's products. In this case, we can define the following fields:

- ID (INTEGER PRIMARY KEY AUTOINCREMENT): represents the unique identifier of the product;
- Name (TEXT NOT NULL): represents the product's name;
- Price (REAL): represents the product's price;
- Quantity (INTEGER): represents the quantity of the product available.

This field definition ensures that each product has a unique and incremental ID, a mandatory name, a price, and a quantity associated with it. Additionally, further rules or constraints can be defined for the fields, such as setting a minimum limit for the price or quantity using the CHECK options.

Properly defining the fields of a table in SQLite is a fundamental step to ensure proper data organization and easy information management. By using available data types and options, it is possible to tailor the table structure to the specific needs of the application and ensure data consistency and integrity. With correct table design, optimal performance can be ensured, and querying and manipulating data can be facilitated.

## 5. Definition of table fields

When creating a table in SQLite, it is essential to carefully define the fields to ensure proper data organization and easy querying. In this article, we will explore in detail the different data types and options available for defining the fields of a table in SQLite.

Before delving into the details of individual fields, it is important to understand the basic concepts regarding table definition in SQLite. Each table consists of rows and columns, and each column represents a field, which can contain data of various types. For each field, a data type must be specified, which determines the type of data that can be stored in that field and the operations that can be performed on it.

The data types supported by SQLite can be divided into different groups, including:

- Numerical: include INTEGER, REAL, and NUMERIC;
- Textual: TEXT and VARCHAR;
- Date/time: DATE, TIME, and

TIMESTAMP.

Each data type has specific characteristics and limitations that should be considered when defining the structure of a table. For example, INTEGER fields can contain integer numerical values, while TEXT fields can contain variable-length text strings.

In addition to the data type, additional options can be specified for the fields, which determine how the data is handled and the validity rules that must be followed. Some of the most common options include:

- PRIMARY KEY: indicates that the field is a primary key, which must be unique for each row of the table and is used to uniquely identify each row;
- AUTOINCREMENT: indicates that the value of the field is automatically generated incrementally for each new row inserted into the table;
- NOT NULL: indicates that the field cannot be NULL and must contain a valid value;
- UNIQUE: indicates that the field must contain unique values for all rows of the table;

- DEFAULT: specifies a default value that is assigned to the field if a value is not specified during data insertion.

By using these options, it is possible to define the fields of a table flexibly and adapt them to the specific needs of the application. For example, if you want to create a user table where the user ID must be unique and incremental, you can define the ID field with the INTEGER type and the PRIMARY KEY and AUTOINCREMENT options.

To further illustrate how to define the fields of a table in SQLite, consider a practical example of a "Products" table containing information about a store's products. In this case, we can define the following fields:

- ID (INTEGER PRIMARY KEY AUTOINCREMENT): represents the unique identifier of the product;
- Name (TEXT NOT NULL): represents the product name;
- Price (REAL): represents the product price;
- Quantity (INTEGER): represents the available quantity of the product.

This field definition ensures that each product has a unique and incremental ID, a required name, a price, and a quantity associated with it. Additionally, further rules or constraints can be defined for the fields, such as setting a minimum limit for the price or quantity, using the CHECK options.

Properly defining the fields of a table in SQLite is a fundamental step to ensure proper data organization and easy information management. By using the available data types and options, it is possible to tailor the table structure to the specific needs of the application and ensure data consistency and integrity. With proper table design, optimal performance can be achieved, and data querying and manipulation operations can be facilitated.

## 6. Modifying the table structure

Modifying the structure of a table in SQLite is a fairly simple operation that can be done using SQL language. Before proceeding with the modification of the table, it is essential to backup the data present so that they can be restored in case of errors or issues during the modification process.

To add a new column to an existing table, you use the command ALTER TABLE followed by the table name and the command ADD COLUMN followed by the name of the new column and the data type it should contain. For example, to add a "email" column of text type to the "users" table, you would execute the following SQL command:

ALTER TABLE users ADD COLUMN email TEXT;

This command will modify the "users" table by adding the new "email" column of text type. It is important to note that adding a new column does not result in the loss of existing data in the table, but simply adds a new column to the existing structure.

To modify the data type of an existing column, you use the command ALTER TABLE followed by the table name and the command MODIFY COLUMN followed by the column name and the new data type it should contain. For example, to change the data type of the "email" column from text to long text (LONGTEXT) in the "users" table, you would execute the following SQL command:

ALTER TABLE users MODIFY COLUMN email LONGTEXT;

This command will modify the structure of the "users" table by changing the data type of the "email" column from text to long text. Again, changing the data type of a column does not result in the loss of existing data in the table, but simply changes the data type of the existing column.

To delete a no longer necessary column, you use the command ALTER TABLE followed by the table name and the command DROP COLUMN followed by the name of the column you want to eliminate. For example, to delete the "email" column from the "users" table, you would execute the following SQL command:

ALTER TABLE users DROP COLUMN email;

With this command, the "email" column will be deleted from the structure of the "users" table. It is important to note that deleting a column results in the loss of data contained in that column, so it is advisable to backup the data before proceeding with the deletion operation.

Furthermore, it is possible to modify the structure of a table by combining multiple operations in a single SQL command. For example, you can add a new column, change the data type of an existing column, and delete a no longer necessary column in a single SQL statement. Here is an example of how you can combine various table structure modification operations:

ALTER TABLE users
ADD COLUMN phone INTEGER,
MODIFY COLUMN email LONGTEXT,
DROP COLUMN address;

With this SQL command, a new "phone" column of integer type will be added to the "users" table, the data type of the "email" column will be changed from text to long text, and finally the "address" column will be deleted from the structure of the "users" table.

In conclusion, modifying the structure of a table in SQLite is a fairly simple operation that can be done using SQL language. It is important to backup data before proceeding with modification operations and to be careful not to lose important data during the process. With the ALTER TABLE commands, you can effectively and quickly add, modify, or delete columns from an existing table, allowing you to adapt the database structure to the needs of the ongoing project.

## 7. Deleting a SQLite table

Before proceeding with the deletion of a table, it is important to ensure that you have the necessary permissions to perform this operation. Make sure you have administrator rights or the necessary privileges to delete a table in the database.

To delete a table from a SQLite database, you can use the SQL command DROP TABLE followed by the name of the table you want to delete. For example, if you want to delete a table named "users", the command to do so would be:

DROP TABLE users;

So, let's say we have a database called "mydatabase.db" and we want to delete the "users" table within this database. Our SQL command would be as follows:

DROP TABLE users;

Once this command is executed, the "users"

table will be deleted from the "mydatabase.db" database and all data within it will be permanently lost. It is important to be cautious when deleting a table, as this operation cannot be undone and the data cannot be recovered once the table has been deleted.

If you want to delete a table only if it exists in the database, you can use the DROP TABLE IF EXISTS command followed by the name of the table you want to delete. This command will prevent errors in case the table does not exist in the database. For example, if you want to delete the "users" table only if it exists in the "mydatabase.db" database, the command would be:

DROP TABLE IF EXISTS users;

This command will check if the "users" table exists in the database before attempting to delete it. If the table exists, it will be deleted. If the table does not exist, the command will be ignored and no error will be generated.

It is important to note that deleting a table

from a SQLite database does not automatically remove any dependencies or references to it within other tables or views in the database. If the table you want to delete is referenced by other tables or views, make sure to handle these dependencies properly before proceeding with the table deletion.

Furthermore, before deleting a table, make sure to perform a full backup of the database to avoid accidental loss of important data. If possible, create a backup copy of the database before proceeding with the deletion of a table to be able to restore the data in case of an error.

In summary, deleting a table from a SQLite database is a simple operation but requires attention and precaution. Make sure you have the necessary permissions, backup the database, and handle dependencies properly before deleting a table. Use the SQL commands DROP TABLE or DROP TABLE IF EXISTS to safely and cautiously delete a table. With proper attention and precautions, it is possible to effectively and risk-free delete a table from a SQLite database.

# 8. SQLite CRUD Operations

CRUD operations (Create, Read, Update, Delete) represent the fundamental actions that can be performed on a database. SQLite is a lightweight and fast database that efficiently supports these operations. In this article, we will explore in detail how to perform CRUD operations in SQLite.

Creating a SQLite database
To start working with SQLite, you need to create a database. To do this, you can use the `sqlite3` command from the command line or a graphical interface like DB Browser for SQLite. For example, to create a database called `mydatabase.db`, simply run the following command from the command line:

```bash
sqlite3 mydatabase.db
```

Once the database is created, you can begin performing CRUD operations.
Create (inserting data)

To insert data into a SQLite table, you use the `INSERT INTO` command. For example, to insert a new record into the `users` table with the values `John Doe` and `john.doe@email.com`, you can run the following SQL command:

```sql
INSERT INTO users (name, email) VALUES ('John Doe', 'john.doe@email.com');
```

This allows you to insert new records into the database.

Read (reading data)
To read data from a SQLite table, you use the `SELECT` command. For example, to retrieve all records from the `users` table, you can run the following SQL command:

```sql
SELECT * FROM users;
```

This command will return all records in the `users` table. You can also specify search conditions to filter the data. For example, to retrieve only the records with the email `john.doe@email.com`:

```sql
SELECT * FROM users WHERE email = 'john.doe@email.com';
```

This allows you to read the data in the database.

Update (updating data)
To update data in a SQLite table, you use the `UPDATE` command. For example, to modify the email of the record with the name `John Doe`:

```sql
UPDATE users SET email = 'john.doe@example.com' WHERE name = 'John Doe';
```

This allows you to update the data in the database.

Delete (deleting data)

To delete data from a SQLite table, you use the `DELETE` command. For example, to delete the record with the email `john.doe@email.com`:

```sql
DELETE FROM users WHERE email = 'john.doe@email.com';
```

This allows you to delete data from the database.

## Conclusion

CRUD operations are essential for managing data within a database. SQLite offers an efficient implementation of these operations, making it a popular choice for mobile and web applications where a lightweight and fast database is needed. Knowing how to perform CRUD operations in SQLite is essential for developing robust and high-performing applications.

## 9.Data Insertion and Data Reading

Data insertion in a SQLite database is done through the use of specific SQL queries that allow inserting new rows into a table. To perform an insertion operation, it is necessary to use the INSERT INTO command followed by the table name and the list of values to insert.

For example, if we want to insert data related to a new user into the "users" table with fields "name" and "surname", we can use the following query:

INSERT INTO users (name, surname) VALUES ('Mario', 'Rossi');

This query will insert a new row into the "users" table with the values "Mario" and "Rossi" in the "name" and "surname" fields respectively.

It is possible to insert multiple rows simultaneously using a single insertion query. For example, to insert multiple users at once, we can use the following syntax:

INSERT INTO users (name, surname)
VALUES
('Mario', 'Rossi'),
('Luigi', 'Verdi'),
('Giovanni', 'Bianchi');

This way, three new rows will be inserted into the "users" table with values corresponding to the "name" and "surname" fields.

Data Reading from SQLite

Once the data has been inserted into the database, it is possible to retrieve it using specific read queries. To perform a reading operation, it is necessary to use the SELECT command followed by the list of fields to retrieve and the reference table.

For example, to read all data related to users in the "users" table, we can use the following query:

SELECT * FROM users;

This query will return all data in the "users" table, including all fields and rows.

It is possible to filter the retrieved data using WHERE clauses that allow specifying search conditions. For example, if we want to retrieve data only related to users with the name "Mario", we can use the following query:

SELECT * FROM users WHERE name = 'Mario';

This query will return only data related to users with the name "Mario".

It is also possible to sort the retrieved data using the ORDER BY clause, which allows specifying the sorting field and direction (ascending or descending). For example, if we want to sort user data by surname in descending order, we can use the following query:

SELECT * FROM users ORDER BY surname DESC;

This query will return user data sorted by surname in descending order.

Optimizing Read Queries

To ensure optimal performance in executing read queries, it is important to consider some best practices and optimizations. Below are some useful tips:

1. Use indexes: creating indexes on fields frequently used in search queries can significantly improve the performance of read queries. Indexes help reduce the time required to retrieve data, improving the overall system efficiency.

2. Limit the retrieved results: when possible, limit the number of retrieved results using the LIMIT clause. Limiting results can reduce query execution time, especially when working with large amounts of data.

3. Use aggregate functions: when performing aggregation operations on data, it is advisable to use aggregate functions provided by SQLite such as COUNT, SUM, AVG, etc. These

functions allow performing complex operations on data efficiently.

4. Use transactions: using transactions can improve the performance of read and write operations on data. Transactions allow managing multiple operations atomically, ensuring data consistency and integrity.

Data insertion and reading in SQLite are fundamental operations for the proper functioning of a data management system. Knowing the best practices and optimizations to efficiently execute queries is essential to ensure optimal performance and effective data management. By following the guidelines and suggestions provided in this article, it will be possible to optimize the performance of data insertion and reading operations in SQLite, ensuring smooth and reliable database operation.

# 10. Updating Data and Deleting Data in SQLite

One of the key features of SQLite is the ability to update and delete data within the database. In this article, we will look at how to perform data updates and data deletions in SQLite.

Updating data in SQLite

To update data in a SQLite table, you can use the SQL UPDATE statement. This command allows you to modify the values of one or more columns within a specific row. For example, if you want to change the value of a "name" column in the "users" table where the ID is equal to 1, you can use the following command:

UPDATE users SET name = 'New Name' WHERE ID = 1;

In this example, we are updating the value of the "name" field in the "users" table where the ID is equal to 1. You can also update multiple columns at the same time using a similar

UPDATE statement like this:

UPDATE users SET name = 'New Name', email = 'new@email.com' WHERE ID = 1;

In this case, we are updating both the "name" and "email" fields in the "users" table where the ID is equal to 1. You can update multiple rows at the same time using a single UPDATE statement. For example, to update the "city" field to "Rome" for all records where the "state" field is equal to "Italy", you can use the following command:

UPDATE users SET city = 'Rome' WHERE state = 'Italy';

This SQL statement will update the "city" field to "Rome" for all records in the "users" table where the "state" field is equal to "Italy". It is important to always define a WHERE clause in the UPDATE statement to avoid inadvertently updating all records in the table.

Deleting data in SQLite

To delete data from a SQLite table, you can

use the SQL DELETE statement. This command allows you to remove one or more rows from a table. For example, to delete a specific row from the "users" table where the ID is equal to 1, you can use the following command:

DELETE FROM users WHERE ID = 1;

In this example, we are deleting the row with the ID equal to 1 from the "users" table. You can also delete multiple rows at the same time using a single DELETE statement. For example, to delete all rows from the "users" table where the "state" field is equal to "Italy", you can use the following command:

DELETE FROM users WHERE state = 'Italy';

This SQL statement will delete all rows from the "users" table where the "state" field is equal to "Italy". Just like with updating data, it is important to always define a WHERE clause in the DELETE statement to avoid inadvertently deleting all records in the table.

Updating and deleting data are common

operations that can be performed in SQLite using the SQL UPDATE and DELETE statements. It is important to exercise caution when performing these operations to avoid making unintentional changes to the database. Additionally, before executing a large-scale update or deletion, it is advisable to backup the database to prevent loss of important data. With proper data management, you can make the most of SQLite's features and create efficient and reliable applications.

## 11. Using SQL commands to create queries

Creating SQL queries is a fundamental part of accessing and managing data within a database. Different SQL commands can be used to create queries and retrieve specific information from stored data.

The main SQL commands used to create queries include SELECT, FROM, WHERE, GROUP BY, HAVING, and ORDER BY. Each command plays a specific role in the query creation process to obtain the desired data.

The SELECT command is the most common and is used to select data from a table or multiple tables within the database. You can specify the fields of interest to include in the query using the SELECT command followed by the desired field names. For example, SELECT First_name, Last_name FROM Employees will only select the First_name and Last_name fields from the Employees table.

The FROM command is used to specify from which tables you want to extract the data. You can specify one or more tables separated by commas to retrieve data from multiple sources. For example, SELECT * FROM Employees, Departments will select all fields from the Employees and Departments tables.

The WHERE command is used to filter data based on certain conditions. Logical operators such as =, <, >, <=, >=, and <> can be used to establish conditions for data filtering. For example, SELECT * FROM Employees WHERE Salary > 50000 will select all employees with a salary greater than 50000.

The GROUP BY command is used to group data based on the values of one or more columns. Aggregation functions such as COUNT, SUM, AVG, and MAX can be used to perform calculations on grouped data. For example, SELECT Department, COUNT(*) FROM Employees GROUP BY Department will return the number of employees for each department.

The HAVING command is used to filter the results of a GROUP BY statement based on certain conditions. It is similar to the WHERE command, but is applied after the data has been aggregated. For example, SELECT Department, COUNT(*) FROM Employees GROUP BY Department HAVING COUNT(*) > 5 will only return departments with more than 5 employees.

Finally, the ORDER BY command is used to sort the data obtained from the query based on the values of one or more columns. You can specify the sorting order using the ASC or DESC keywords. For example, SELECT * FROM Employees ORDER BY Salary DESC will order employees based on salary in descending order.

Using SQL commands to create queries is essential for extracting specific information from data stored in a database. Knowing how to correctly use the SELECT, FROM, WHERE, GROUP BY, HAVING, and ORDER BY commands will allow you to retrieve the desired data effectively and efficiently.

## 12. Using SQLite built-in functions

SQLite offers the ability to use built-in functions to perform complex operations directly within SQL queries. These functions are very useful for performing specific tasks such as mathematical operations, format conversions, string manipulations, and much more.

SQLite's built-in functions are divided into different categories such as mathematical functions, string functions, date/time functions, and aggregation functions. Each of these categories offers a wide range of useful functions to perform specific operations.

SQLite's mathematical functions allow you to perform mathematical operations such as addition, subtraction, multiplication, division, square root, absolute value, rounding, and much more directly within SQL queries. These functions make it easier and faster to perform complex calculations on data in the database.

SQLite's string functions allow you to perform string manipulation operations such as concatenation, substring search, string replacement, case conversion, and much more. These functions are very useful for manipulating and formatting data to make it more readable and relevant for the application.

SQLite's date/time functions allow you to perform operations on date/time data such as format conversions, adding or subtracting days, months, and years, extracting parts of a date (such as day, month, year, hour, minute, and second), and much more. These functions are essential for efficiently managing temporal data in the database.

SQLite's aggregation functions allow you to perform aggregation operations such as sum, average, count, maximum value, and minimum value on a set of data. These functions are useful for obtaining statistics and aggregated information on data in the database.

With SQLite's built-in functions, you can perform complex operations directly within SQL queries without having to rely on external scripting or complex procedures. This makes SQLite an ideal choice for applications that require a lightweight and performant database with the ability to perform advanced operations on data.

In conclusion, using SQLite's built-in functions offers numerous advantages as it allows you to efficiently and quickly perform complex operations directly within SQL queries. These functions are extremely useful for manipulating and analyzing data in the database to obtain relevant and useful information for the application.

# 13. Using subquery and JOIN operations

SQLite is a lightweight and reliable database management system that offers a wide range of features for data management. One of the most useful features of SQLite is the ability to use subquery and JOIN operations to optimize queries and obtain more precise and comprehensive results.

Subqueries are internal queries that are executed within a main query. They allow filtering results based on specific conditions and obtaining specific information from multiple tables without having to execute separate queries. Subqueries can be used in various contexts, such as WHERE, HAVING, and JOIN clauses, to perform complex operations and obtain more detailed results.

JOIN operations, on the other hand, allow combining data from multiple tables to obtain related information. JOIN operations include INNER JOIN, LEFT JOIN, RIGHT JOIN, and FULL JOIN, each with different ways of combining data. By using JOIN operations, you can obtain more complete and detailed results by combining table data based on specific correlation conditions.

SQLite supports a wide range of features for using subquery and JOIN operations, allowing users to execute complex queries and optimize database performance. Below are some examples of how to use subquery and JOIN operations in SQLite to obtain more precise and comprehensive results.

Example of using subquery in SQLite:

Suppose you have two tables, "customers" and "orders", and you want to get a list of customers who have placed at least one order. You can use a subquery in the WHERE clause to filter results based on the presence of orders for each customer:

```
SELECT *
FROM customers
WHERE id IN (SELECT DISTINCT customer_id FROM orders);
```

In this case, the subquery is executed for each row of the "customers" table and returns the IDs of customers who have placed at least one order. The WHERE clause filters the results of the main query based on the ID returned by the subquery, allowing you to get only customers who have placed orders.

Example of using JOIN operations in SQLite:

Suppose you have two tables, "customers" and "orders", and you want to get a list of customers with their respective orders. You can use an INNER JOIN operation to combine data from the two tables based on the customer ID:

```
SELECT customers.name, orders.product
FROM customers
INNER JOIN orders ON customers.id = orders.customer_id;
```

In this case, the JOIN operation combines data from the "customers" and "orders" tables based on the customer ID, returning the customer's name and the ordered product for each match found. By using an INNER JOIN, you will only get results where there is a match between the data in the two tables.

SQLite offers various features for using subquery and JOIN operations, allowing users to execute complex queries and obtain more precise and comprehensive results. By effectively using subquery and JOIN operations, you can optimize queries and improve database performance, allowing you to efficiently manage data and obtain more detailed and relevant information.

# 14. Introduction to transactions and transaction execution in SQLite

SQLite is a lightweight and versatile database management system that supports a wide range of features, including transaction management. Transactions are essential to ensure data integrity in a database, allowing users to perform complex operations involving multiple queries in a consistent and secure manner.

Transactions in SQLite are managed using the concepts of commit and rollback. When a transaction is initiated, all subsequent operations are considered part of that transaction. A transaction can be committed or rolled back depending on the outcome of the operations within it.

To initiate a transaction in SQLite, the BEGIN TRANSACTION command can be used. Once a transaction is initiated, all necessary operations can be performed, and then the decision to commit or rollback the transaction can be made. To commit a transaction, the COMMIT command must be used, while the

ROLLBACK command can be used to rollback the transaction.

Transactions in SQLite offer a high level of flexibility and control to developers. For example, a transaction can be implicitly initiated by simply executing a series of queries without using the BEGIN TRANSACTION command. However, it is important to note that in the case of an error during an implicit transaction, all operations performed up to that point will be rolled back unless a rollback is explicitly executed.

Additionally, SQLite supports exclusive mode transactions and autocommit mode transactions. In exclusive mode, a transaction is manually managed using the BEGIN TRANSACTION, COMMIT, and ROLLBACK commands. In autocommit mode, each individual query is treated as a separate transaction and is automatically committed at the end of the operation.

It is essential to understand the concept of transactions in SQLite to ensure data consistency and integrity in the database. By correctly using transactions, issues such as data loss or data inconsistency due to simultaneous operations or code errors can be avoided.

Transactions in SQLite are a powerful tool for managing complex operations in the database safely and consistently. With a proper understanding and application of transactions, the stability and reliability of the SQLite database can be guaranteed in any situation.

## 15. Commit and rollback of transactions in SQLite

Transactions are a fundamental part of data management in a SQLite database. They allow grouping a set of operations into a single logical unit that can be executed atomically, ensuring that all changes are either applied correctly or none of them are applied.

SQLite supports the concept of transactions through two key statements: COMMIT and ROLLBACK. These commands allow confirming or canceling the changes made during an ongoing transaction.

The COMMIT command is used to definitively confirm transactions, making the changes permanent in the database. Once COMMIT is executed, all operations within the transaction are applied, and resources are released. On the other hand, the ROLLBACK command cancels all changes made during the transaction and restores the previous state of the involved resources. This command is used to cancel invalid transactions or to manage any errors that occur during operation execution.

SQLite automatically manages transactions in autocommit mode, meaning that every single modification operation carried out on the database is considered a separate transaction. However, it is possible to manually start and end a transaction using BEGIN TRANSACTION and END TRANSACTION commands if you wish to explicitly group multiple operations into one transaction.

Furthermore, SQLite supports multiple transactions mode, allowing for nesting transactions within other transactions. This provides greater flexibility in managing complex database operations and helps to maintain data consistency in more intricate scenarios.

Transactions are a fundamental concept to ensure data consistency and integrity in a SQLite database. By appropriately using COMMIT and ROLLBACK commands, you can ensure that changes are applied correctly, and any errors are effectively handled. The ability to start, confirm, and cancel transactions explicitly provides granular control over database operations and allows for efficient management of complex transactions.

# 16. Transaction Management in case of error in SQLite

Transaction management in case of error in SQLite is a fundamental aspect to consider when developing an application that uses this relational database. Transactions are a series of operations that must be executed atomically, meaning that either all of them are completed successfully or none of them are carried out.

SQLite offers the possibility to manage transactions with the BEGIN TRANSACTION command, which marks the beginning of a transaction, and the COMMIT command, which marks its successful completion. In case an error occurs during the execution of a transaction, it is important to be able to handle the situation in order to avoid data inconsistency issues.

When errors occur during a transaction in SQLite, the ROLLBACK command can be used to undo all the changes made up to that point and restore the previous state of the database. This ensures data integrity and prevents potential negative consequences on the application's operation.

It is important to note that error handling during transactions in SQLite should be supported by adequate control of the code execution flow, in order to ensure the correct sequence of operations to be performed in case of error. Additionally, it is advisable to use smaller and more atomic transactions possible, in order to minimize the risk of errors and simplify transaction management.

An example of transaction management in case of error in SQLite could be the following:

```python
import sqlite3

conn = sqlite3.connect('database.db')
cursor = conn.cursor()

try:
    cursor.execute('BEGIN TRANSACTION')

    # Perform database operations that need to
```

be executed within the transaction here

```
    cursor.execute('COMMIT')
except sqlite3.Error:
    cursor.execute('ROLLBACK')
    # Handle the error appropriately here

conn.close()
```

In this example, a connection to the database is opened and a cursor is created to execute database operations within the transaction. The BEGIN TRANSACTION command is then executed to start the transaction. If an error occurs during the execution of operations, the ROLLBACK command is executed to undo the changes and restore the previous state of the database. Finally, the connection to the database is closed.

Proper transaction management in case of error in SQLite is essential to ensure data integrity and the correct operation of the application. By using BEGIN TRANSACTION, COMMIT, and ROLLBACK commands appropriately and supporting the code with proper control of the execution flow, transactions in SQLite can be successfully managed and potential data consistency issues can be prevented.

## 17. Database Backup Database Restore from a Backup

Database backup and restore are essential to ensure the security and integrity of the data contained within it. SQLite, being a serverless database, offers simple but effective procedures for performing data backup and restore.

Backing up the database in SQLite can be done using various approaches, such as the .backup command or direct copying of the database file. In both cases, it is important for the database not to be in use during the backup to avoid potential data loss or corruption of the database itself.

To perform a database backup using the .backup command, you can use an administration tool like SQLiteStudio or SQLiteManager. These tools offer an intuitive user interface that allows you to easily backup the database with a few clicks.

Alternatively, you can make a direct copy of

the database file using the cp command in Unix/Linux environments or the copy command in Windows environments. This approach is useful when you want to quickly and easily create backup copies of the database.

Regardless of the chosen approach, it is important to store the database backup in a secure location, preferably on an external storage device or a reliable cloud service. Additionally, it is advisable to regularly backup the database to ensure data security.

Once the database backup is created, you can restore the data in case of loss or damage to the original database. To restore the database from a backup, you can use the .restore command in SQLiteStudio or SQLiteManager. This command allows you to select the backup file to restore and perform the operation quickly and easily.

Alternatively, you can restore the database using the cp command in Unix/Linux environments or the copy command in Windows environments to replace the current database file with the backup file. It is important to be cautious during this operation to avoid accidental data overwrite.

Before proceeding with the database restore from a backup, it is advisable to verify that the backup file is intact and undamaged. In case of issues during the restore, you can revert to a previous backup or use another data recovery method.

Database backup and restore in SQLite are crucial operations to ensure data security and integrity. By using the correct tools and procedures, you can create reliable backup copies and efficiently restore data in case of emergencies. Remember to regularly backup the database and store backup copies in a secure location to protect data from potential loss and damage.

# 18. Backup Creation
# Backup File Management in SQLite

Creating backups and managing backup files in SQLite are essential procedures to ensure that critical data is protected from accidental loss or database damage. SQLite is a lightweight and fast database commonly used in mobile applications, web browsers, and other embedded systems. Although SQLite is designed to be stable and reliable, it is still important to have a backup and restore plan in place to protect the data.

Creating backups in SQLite can be done in various ways, including using the "backup" command and third-party tools. One common option is to use SQLite's "backup" command to create a copy of the database on disk or in another location. This command copies both the database contents and its indexes and other metadata. For example, the command `sqlite3 db.sqlite .backup backup.db` creates a copy of the `db.sqlite` database called `backup.db`.

Another option for creating backups in SQLite

is to use third-party libraries such as sqlitebck. These libraries offer advanced functionality for creating backups and restoring data. For example, sqlitebck offers the ability to create incremental backups, which are backups that only contain changes made to the database since the last backup.

Managing backup files in SQLite is equally important. It is essential to keep track of created backups and ensure they are available when needed. It is advisable to maintain multiple backups in different locations to avoid complete data loss in case of hardware failure or natural disaster. It is also important to regularly verify the integrity of backup files to ensure they are usable when needed.

To effectively manage backup files in SQLite, it is advisable to use a combination of automated and manual procedures. For example, you can schedule automatic backups using a script that regularly runs the SQLite "backup" command and stores backups in a dedicated folder. It is also advisable to generate periodic verification reports to ensure backups are complete and intact.

In the event of data loss or database damage, the procedure for restoring backup files in SQLite is essential. To restore a database from a backup, you can use the SQLite "restore" command to copy data from the backup to the main database. For example, the command `sqlite3 db.sqlite .restore backup.db` restores the `db.sqlite` database from the `backup.db` backup.

Furthermore, it is advisable to regularly test the backup restoration process to ensure it is functional and data is properly restored in case of an emergency. It is important to consider the time required for data restoration and plan accordingly to minimize downtime.

Creating backups and managing backup files in SQLite are fundamental practices to ensure the security and integrity of critical data. It is important to plan and implement effective backup procedures to protect data from accidental loss or database damage. With proper backup file management, the risk of data loss can be minimized, and system operational continuity can be ensured.

## 19. Using Indexes to Improve Performance in SQLite

Indexes in SQLite are powerful tools that allow for more efficient access and retrieval of data. An index is a data structure that is created on one or more columns of a table to speed up the process of searching for records. When an index is created on a table, SQLite creates an ordered copy of the indexed columns in a way that makes accessing the corresponding data faster.

There are different types of indexes that can be created in SQLite, including unique indexes, composite indexes, and partial indexes. Unique indexes ensure that values in the indexed columns are unique, while composite indexes are created on multiple columns to improve query performance involving multiple columns. On the other hand, partial indexes are created on subsets of rows in a table and can improve the performance of specific queries.

To create an index in SQLite, the following

syntax is used:

```sql
CREATE INDEX index_name ON table_name (column1, column2, ...);
```

In the example above, "index_name" is the name of the index you want to create, "table_name" is the name of the table on which you want to create the index, and "column1, column2, ..." are the columns of the table on which you want to create the index.

Once an index is created, it can be used to speed up queries involving the indexed columns. For example, if you have an SQL statement like this:

```sql
SELECT * FROM table WHERE column = 'value';
```

SQLite will use the index created on the "column" column to quickly search for records matching the specified value.

It is important to note that using indexes is not always advantageous and can result in additional overhead during insertion, update, or deletion of records. Before creating an index, it is important to carefully evaluate the queries you want to optimize and consider whether using an index will actually lead to performance improvements.

Additionally, it is essential to keep in mind that SQLite supports a maximum number of indexes per table. Exceeding this limit can result in performance and memory management issues.

To check which indexes exist on a table and which indexes are being used by a query, you can use the "EXPLAIN QUERY PLAN" command in SQLite. This command provides detailed information on the query optimization performed by the SQLite engine, allowing you to identify any shortcomings in index usage.

In conclusion, using indexes in SQLite is an effective way to improve query performance and optimize data access. However, it is important to carefully evaluate when and how to create indexes to ensure that actual performance benefits are achieved. With proper index design and ongoing evaluation of database performance, you can maximize the efficiency and reliability of your SQLite-based applications.

## 20. Using cache to optimize queries
## Query Optimization in SQLite

SQLite is a lightweight and fast database management system that supports many standard SQL features. However, due to its lightweight and serverless nature, it can sometimes become slow when working with large datasets or complex queries. To optimize queries in SQLite and improve database performance, you can use cache.

Cache in SQLite consists of two main components: page cache and lookaside cache. The page cache stores database page blocks in memory to avoid loading them from disk every time they are accessed. This helps reduce data access times and improve overall database performance. The lookaside cache, on the other hand, stores table and query metadata to reduce latency in complex queries.

To optimize queries in SQLite using cache, you can follow several approaches. The first step is to configure the page cache size optimally. The default page cache size in

SQLite is 2 MB, but you can increase or decrease it depending on the database needs. Increasing the page cache size can improve database performance, but it is important to be careful not to use too much memory, as it could cause an increase in resource consumption.

Another way to optimize queries in SQLite is to use the PRAGMA cache_size statement to set the page cache size. For example, you can run the following SQL command to set the page cache to 4 MB:

PRAGMA cache_size=4000;

This statement would set the page cache size to 4 MB, which can help improve database performance. It is important to note that this setting is not permanent and will be reset when the database is closed and reopened.

Furthermore, you can use the PRAGMA cache_spill statement to enable or disable page cache spill over. Page cache spill over occurs when the cache is full and data needs to be written to disk. Disabling page cache spill over can help improve database performance by avoiding costly disk write operations. To enable page cache spill over, you can run the following SQL command:

PRAGMA cache_spill=OFF;

It is important to keep in mind that disabling page cache spill over may result in increased memory usage, so it is important to carefully monitor system resources.

In addition to using page cache, you can also leverage the lookaside cache to optimize queries in SQLite. The lookaside cache stores table and query metadata to reduce latency in complex queries. To enable the lookaside cache, you can use the PRAGMA default_cache_size statement to set the lookaside cache size. For example, you can run the following SQL command to set the lookaside cache size to 4096 bytes:

PRAGMA default_cache_size=4096;

It is important to note that the lookaside cache is shared among all database connections, so it is important not to set a size that is too large, which could lead to excessive resource consumption.

Finally, to further optimize queries in SQLite, you can use indexes to speed up data retrieval. Indexes are data structures used to speed up record search within a table and can be used to reduce query execution times. To create an index in SQLite, you can use the CREATE INDEX statement followed by the index name and the table and fields on which to create the index. For example, you can create an index on the "name" field of the "users" table with the following SQL command:

CREATE INDEX idx_name ON users(name);

Creating indexes on columns that are frequently used in queries can help improve database performance by reducing record search times.

By using cache in SQLite, you can optimize queries and improve database performance. By optimizing the page cache and lookaside cache size, enabling page cache spill over, and creating indexes on commonly used query columns, you can reduce data access times and improve query execution speed. It is important to test and closely monitor database performance after making cache changes to ensure that there are actual improvements and no undesired effects on overall system performance.

# 21. Security

Database protection is a critical part of ensuring security and integrity of sensitive data. One of the main methods to protect a database is using passwords to control access by authorized users. Additionally, managing user permissions and protecting sensitive data are crucial to ensure that only authorized individuals can access sensitive information.

1. Using passwords to protect the database:

One of the first lines of defense to protect a database is using passwords to control user access. Passwords should be complex and unique for each user to ensure that only authorized individuals can access the database. It is important to use a combination of upper and lowercase letters, numbers, and special characters to make passwords more secure. Additionally, it is advisable to regularly change passwords and not share them with others.

To adequately protect the database, it is

advisable to use a strong password policy that requires a minimum length and a mix of different characters. Furthermore, it is recommended to use encryption to protect passwords in the database so that even if the database is compromised, the passwords remain secure.

2. User permission management:

Managing user permissions is essential to ensure that only authorized individuals can access sensitive information in the database. It is important to define clear roles and responsibilities for users and assign them necessary permissions to carry out their tasks without granting unauthorized access to sensitive information.

One of the best ways to manage user permissions is to use a role-based model, where different roles with different privileges are defined and users are assigned to one or more roles based on their responsibilities. Additionally, it is advisable to regularly monitor and audit user activity to identify any anomalies or suspicious behavior.

3. Protection of sensitive data:

Protecting sensitive data is crucial to ensure that sensitive information in the database is safe from unauthorized access. To protect sensitive data, it is advisable to use encryption to protect data both in transit and at rest. Additionally, implementing role-based access controls is recommended to ensure that only authorized individuals can access sensitive information.

To protect sensitive data in the database, it is also important to implement physical security measures, such as physically securing servers where sensitive data is stored and ensuring that only authorized individuals can physically access the servers. Furthermore, using anonymization and pseudonymization techniques to protect sensitive data and ensure user privacy is recommended.

4. Improving database security in SQLite:

SQLite is a lightweight and fast database widely used in mobile applications and other high-performance applications. To improve database security in SQLite, it is advisable to implement the following security measures:

- Use passwords to control access to the database
- Encrypt sensitive data in the database
- Implement role-based access controls
- Regularly monitor and audit user activity
- Implement physical security measures to protect servers where the database is stored

Database protection is an ongoing process that requires collaboration between development teams, security teams, and authorized users to ensure that sensitive information is adequately protected. By using secure passwords, managing user permissions, and protecting sensitive data, it is possible to enhance database security and reduce the risk of security breaches.

## 22. Error handling

Error handling is a fundamental aspect in the development of any application or software that interfaces with a database. Errors can occur at different stages of the communication process with the database, and it is therefore important to handle them properly to ensure the security and reliability of the system.

1. Connection error handling

One of the most common problems that can occur during interaction with a database is a connection error. This can be caused by various factors, such as network issues, configuration errors, or server overload.

To properly handle connection errors, you can implement techniques for automatic retry of the connection. This way, if the connection is lost, the system can automatically attempt to reestablish it without the user having to intervene manually. It is also important to handle exceptions that may be thrown in case of a connection error, in order to provide the user with clear and understandable feedback on the error that occurred.

2. SQL syntax error handling

Another common type of error that can occur during interaction with a database is an SQL syntax error. This type of error can be caused by a variety of reasons, such as a malformed query, a typo in the SQL syntax, or an attempt to execute an unauthorized operation.

To properly handle SQL syntax errors, it is important to validate the queries entered by the user before executing them on the database. This way, any errors in the SQL syntax can be detected, and clear feedback can be provided to the user about the error made. Additionally, it is advisable to log SQL syntax errors so that they can be analyzed and corrected to prevent them from occurring again in the future.

## 3. Transaction error handling

Another crucial aspect in handling database errors is managing transaction errors. Transactions in a database are essential to ensure data consistency and integrity, so it is important to properly handle any errors that may occur during the execution of a transaction.

If an error occurs during a transaction, it is essential to properly handle the rollback of the transaction to undo the changes made to the database and restore the previous state. Additionally, it is important to provide the user with clear feedback on the error that occurred and the steps to follow to resolve it appropriately.

## 4. Recovering from database errors in SQLite

SQLite is one of the most widely used database management systems in the world, so it is important to handle any errors that may occur during interaction with this system properly.

To handle database errors in SQLite, you can use the error handling functions provided by the system. For example, you can use the sqlite3_errmsg() function to obtain a detailed error string in case of a database error. You can also set up a custom error handler using the sqlite3_config() function to handle errors specifically and provide the user with clear feedback on the error that occurred.

In conclusion, error handling is a fundamental aspect in the design and development of an application that interfaces with a database. It is important to properly handle connection, SQL syntax, transaction, and database errors to ensure the security and reliability of the system and provide the user with an optimal and hassle-free user experience.

## 23. Practical Examples in SQLite

Some practical examples of how to use SQLite to manage data in different situations.

1. Database and Table Creation:

To start, you need to create an SQLite database and the related tables to store the data. For example, suppose you want to create a database to manage a list of contacts. Here's how you could do it:

```sql
CREATE TABLE contacts (
    id INTEGER PRIMARY KEY AUTOINCREMENT,
    first_name TEXT,
    last_name TEXT,
    phone TEXT
);
```

In this case, we have created a table called `contacts` with four columns: `id` (primary key), `first_name`, `last_name`, and `phone`.

2. Data Insertion:

Once the database and tables are created, we can start inserting data. Using the `INSERT INTO` command, we can add new contacts to the `contacts` table. Here's an example of how you could do it:

```sql
INSERT INTO contacts (first_name, last_name, phone) VALUES ('Mario', 'Rossi', '123456789');
INSERT INTO contacts (first_name, last_name, phone) VALUES ('Paolo', 'Verdi', '987654321');
```

With these commands, we have added two contacts to the `contacts` table.

3. Data Viewing:

Once the data is inserted, we can view it using the `SELECT` command. For example, if we want to view all the contacts in the database, we can do this:

```sql
SELECT * FROM contacts;
```

This command will return all the contacts in the `contacts` table with their information (first name, last name, and phone number).

4. Data Update:

You can update the data in the database using the `UPDATE` command. For example, if we wanted to update the phone number of a contact, we could do this:

```sql
UPDATE contacts SET phone = '999999999' WHERE id = 1;
```

This command will modify the phone number of the contact with `id` equal to 1.

5. Data Deletion:

Finally, you can delete data from the database using the `DELETE` command. For example, if we wanted to delete a contact from the `contacts` table, we could do this:

```sql
DELETE FROM contacts WHERE id = 2;
```

This command will delete the contact with `id` equal to 2 from the `contacts` table.

In short, SQLite offers a wide range of features for managing data in a local database. It is easy to use and very efficient, making it a popular choice among developers for various applications. I hope these practical examples have been helpful in understanding how to use SQLite to effectively manage data.

## 24. Basic Glossary

SQLite is a popular lightweight, open source, and completely self-contained relational database management system. It is designed to be fast, reliable, and easy to use, making it a common choice for mobile applications, embedded devices, web browsers, and other applications that require simple and efficient data management. This glossary will provide an overview of the concepts and key terms used in SQLite.

1. Database: A database in SQLite is a file or a series of files that contain tables, indexes, views, and other database objects. Multiple databases can be used in a single SQLite application.

2. Table: A table is a collection of rows organized in columns that represent related data. Each table in a database has a unique name and a schema that defines the structure of the table, including column names, data types, and other properties.

3. Schema: The schema of a table defines its structure, including column names, column data types, data integrity constraints, and other properties. The schema of a table can be modified using SQL language.

4. Column: A column in an SQLite table represents a single data field and has a unique name and an associated data type, which can be INTEGER, REAL, TEXT, BLOB, or NULL.

5. Data type: SQLite supports various data types, including INTEGER for integer numbers, REAL for floating-point numbers, TEXT for text strings, BLOB for binary data, and NULL for null values.

6. Primary key: A primary key is a field or a set of fields in a table that ensures the uniqueness of each row and provides an efficient way to retrieve data from the table. In SQLite, the primary key is usually defined using the PRIMARY KEY constraint.

7. Foreign key: A foreign key is a field or a set of fields in a table that establishes a

relationship between two tables. In SQLite, the foreign key is usually defined using the FOREIGN KEY constraint.

8. Index: An index is a data structure that speeds up search and sorting operations on a table. In SQLite, indexes can be created on one or more columns using the CREATE INDEX command.

9. Transaction: A transaction is a series of database operations that must be executed as a single atomic unit. In SQLite, transactions are used to ensure data consistency and integrity.

10. Integrity constraint: An integrity constraint is a rule that enforces data restrictions in a table to ensure data consistency and integrity. In SQLite, primary key constraints, foreign key constraints, and other constraints can be created using SQL language.

11. Trigger: A trigger is an SQL statement that is automatically executed when a specific condition occurs on a table. In SQLite, triggers can be created using the CREATE TRIGGER command.

12. View: A view is a predefined query that defines a specific view of data in one or more tables. In SQLite, virtual views can be created using the CREATE VIEW command.

13. Function: A function is an SQL statement that returns a value based on input parameters. Custom functions can be created in SQLite using the CREATE FUNCTION command.

14. Stored procedure: A stored procedure is a block of SQL code that can be executed repeatedly to perform complex operations on the database. SQLite does not support stored procedures like other DBMS.

15. Backup and restore: SQLite supports database backup and restore using the ATTACH DATABASE command to link a backup database to a main database, and the BACKUP DATABASE command to perform a full backup of the database.

16. Query optimization: SQLite provides query optimization using indexes, query caching, and other techniques to improve query performance on large datasets.

17. SQLite shell: The SQLite shell is a command-line interface that allows users to run SQL commands directly on an SQLite database and view results in real-time.

18. SQLite Studio: SQLite Studio is a graphical application that provides an intuitive user interface for managing SQLite databases, including creating and modifying tables, views, triggers, and functions.

19. SQLite Manager: SQLite Manager is an extension for Firefox that provides a graphical interface for managing SQLite databases directly from the web browser, allowing users to run queries, view data, and modify the database.

20. SQLite.NET: SQLite.NET is a wrapper

for SQLite that provides a .NET library for accessing SQLite databases from applications written in C# or other .NET languages. SQLite.NET offers advanced features such as support for transactions, indexes, and other SQLite functionalities.

21. SQLiteSwift: SQLiteSwift is a library for Swift that provides an interface for accessing SQLite databases from iOS and macOS applications written in Swift. SQLiteSwift simplifies data access and transaction management using an intuitive Swift syntax.

22. SQLiteOpenHelper: SQLiteOpenHelper is a support class provided by Android for managing SQLite databases on Android devices. SQLiteOpenHelper simplifies the creation, updating, and version management of SQLite databases using methods such as onCreate() and onUpgrade().

23. SQLiteOpenHelper: SQLiteOpenHelper is a commonly used class in the context of Android application development. This class facilitates the creation and updating operations of a SQLite database in an Android

application.

24. SQLiteManager: SQLiteManager is an administration and development tool for SQLite databases, available as a desktop application or as a web browser extension. SQLiteManager offers features for creating databases, managing tables, and viewing data in an intuitive way.

25. SQLite Browser: SQLite Browser is an open-source desktop application that allows users to view and modify data in a SQLite database, including creating tables, creating indexes, and executing SQL queries.

26. SQLite Expert: SQLite Expert is a powerful administration and development tool for SQLite databases that offers advanced features such as creating visual schemas, importing and exporting data, and managing database performance.

27. SQLite Python: SQLite Python is a Python module that provides an interface for accessing SQLite databases from Python scripts. SQLite Python simplifies database

connection, query execution, and data management using methods such as cursor() and execute().

28. SQLite C API: The SQLite C API is a C programming interface that allows developers to directly access the SQLite database engine using predefined C functions. The SQLite C API provides full control over all SQLite features, including database creation and management.

29. SQLite .NET API: The SQLite .NET API is a .NET programming interface that allows developers to access SQLite databases from applications written in C# or other .NET languages. The SQLite .NET API provides a more intuitive and easier-to-use interface compared to the SQLite C API.

30. SQLite Java API: The SQLite Java API is a Java programming interface that allows developers to access SQLite databases from applications written in Java. The SQLite Java API simplifies database connection, query execution, and data management using

methods such as getConnection() and executeQuery().

31. SQL: SQL, Structured Query Language, is the standard language used to interact with relational databases, including SQLite. SQL provides a set of commands for creating, modifying, and querying tables, views, triggers, and other database objects.

32. CREATE TABLE: The CREATE TABLE command is used to create a new table in a SQLite database with specific columns, data types, and integrity constraints. For example, CREATE TABLE tablename (column1 INT, column2 TEXT, PRIMARY KEY (column1)).

33. INSERT INTO: The INSERT INTO command is used to insert new data rows into an existing table in a SQLite database. For example, INSERT INTO tablename (column1, column2) VALUES ('value1', 'value2').

34. SELECT: The SELECT command is used

to retrieve data from a table or views in a SQLite database based on specific conditions. For example, SELECT * FROM tablename WHERE column1 = 'value'.

35. UPDATE: The UPDATE command is used to modify existing data in a table in a SQLite database based on specific conditions. For example, UPDATE tablename SET column1 = 'newvalue' WHERE column2 = 'value'.

36. DELETE: The DELETE command is used to delete data rows from a table in a SQLite database based on specific conditions. For example, DELETE FROM tablename WHERE column1 = 'value'.

37. ALTER TABLE: The ALTER TABLE command is used to modify the structure of an existing table in a SQLite database, including adding, modifying, or deleting columns. For example, ALTER TABLE tablename ADD column3 INT.

38. DROP TABLE: The DROP TABLE

command is used to delete an existing table from a SQLite database along with all associated data and indexes. For example, DROP TABLE tablename.

39. PRAGMA: The PRAGMA command is used to perform administration and configuration operations on a SQLite database, including viewing and modifying configuration settings. For example, PRAGMA table_info(tablename).

40. ATTACH DATABASE: The ATTACH DATABASE command is used to attach a backup database or additional database to a main database in SQLite to allow for inter-database query operations. For example, ATTACH DATABASE 'backup.db' AS backup.

41. BACKUP DATABASE: The BACKUP

DATABASE command is used to perform a full backup copy of a SQLite database to a new file or a linked backup database. For example, BACKUP DATABASE 'main.db' TO 'backup.db'.

42. UNION: The UNION operator is used to combine the results of two or more SQL queries into a single result set without duplicates. For example, SELECT * FROM table1 UNION SELECT * FROM table2.
43. JOIN: The JOIN operator is used to combine data from two or more tables based on a correlation condition between the columns of the tables. Types of JOIN include INNER JOIN, LEFT JOIN, RIGHT JOIN, and FULL JOIN.

44. INNER JOIN: INNER JOIN combines data from two tables based on a correlation condition between the columns of the tables, returning only rows that have a valid match between the tables.

45. LEFT JOIN: LEFT JOIN combines data

from two tables based on a correlation condition between the columns of the tables, returning all rows from the left table and the corresponding rows from the right table.

46. RIGHT JOIN: RIGHT JOIN combines data from two tables based on a correlation condition between the columns of the tables, returning all rows from the right table and the corresponding rows from the left table.

47. FULL JOIN: FULL JOIN combines data from two tables based on a correlation condition between the columns of the tables, returning all rows from both tables, matching or not.

48. GROUP BY: The GROUP BY command is used together with the aggregation function to group data based on one or more columns and calculate aggregate values for each group. For example, SELECT col1, SUM(col2) FROM tablename GROUP BY col1.

49. HAVING: The HAVING command is

used together with the GROUP BY command to filter groups of data that satisfy certain conditions. For example, SELECT col1, SUM(col2) FROM tablename GROUP BY col1 HAVING SUM(col2) > 100.

50. ORDER BY: The ORDER BY command is used to sort the data retrieved from an SQL query based on one or more columns in either ascending or descending order. For example, SELECT * FROM tablename ORDER BY col1 asc, col2 desc.

51. LIMIT: The LIMIT command is used to limit the number of rows retrieved from an SQL query in SQLite based on a specified upper limit. For example, SELECT * FROM tablename LIMIT 10.

52. OFFSET: The OFFSET command is used together with the LIMIT command to specify the number of rows to skip at the beginning of an SQL query in SQLite. For example, SELECT * FROM tablename LIMIT 10 OFFSET 5.

53. AUTOINCREMENT: The AUTOINCREMENT option is used to specify

that an INTEGER column in a SQLite table should automatically increment values for each row inserted into the table.

54. PRIMARY KEY: The PRIMARY KEY constraint is used to define a primary key in a SQLite table that ensures the uniqueness of each row and provides an efficient way to retrieve data from the table. For example, CREATE TABLE tablename (col1 INT PRIMARY KEY).

55. FOREIGN KEY: The FOREIGN KEY constraint is used to define a foreign key in a SQLite table that establishes a relationship between two tables. For example, CREATE TABLE tablename1 (col1 INT, col2 INT, FOREIGN KEY (col2) REFERENCES tablename2(col3)).

56. UNIQUE: The UNIQUE constraint is used to enforce the uniqueness of values in a column or set of columns in a SQLite table. For example, CREATE TABLE tablename (col1 INT UNIQUE, col2 TEXT, col3 REAL).

57. CHECK: The CHECK constraint is used to enforce specific conditions on a column or set of columns in a SQLite table. For example, CREATE TABLE tablename (col1 INT, col2 TEXT, CHECK (col1 > 0)).

58. TRIGGER: The CREATE TRIGGER command is used to define a trigger in a SQLite table that is automatically executed when a certain condition is met. For example, CREATE TRIGGER triggername AFTER INSERT ON tablename FOR EACH ROW BEGIN UPDATE tablename SET col1 = col1 + 1 WHERE col2 = NEW.col2; END.

59. VIEW: The CREATE VIEW command is used to create a view in SQLite defined by a predefined SQL query that defines a specific visualization of data in one or more tables. For example, CREATE VIEW viewname AS SELECT col1, col2 FROM tablename WHERE col1 > 0.

60. FUNCTION: The CREATE FUNCTION command is used to define a custom function

in SQLite that returns a value based on input parameters. For example, CREATE FUNCTION functionname(param1 INT, param2 TEXT) RETURNS INT AS BEGIN RETURN param1 + LENGTH(param2); END.

61. Bubble Sort: Bubble Sorting is a simple sorting method where elements are compared and swapped one at a time until the entire sequence is sorted in either ascending or descending order.

62. Quick Sort: Quick Sorting is a sorting algorithm where elements are divided into sub-lists using a pivot element and then recursively sorted until the entire sequence is sorted.

63. Merge Sort: Merge Sorting is a divide and conquer sorting algorithm where the sequence is divided into two halves, sorted separately, and then merged together in sorted order.

64. Insertion Sort: Insertion Sorting is a sorting algorithm where elements are inserted

one at a time into the sorted sequence, shifting larger elements to make space for the new element.

65. Selection Sort: Selection Sorting is a sorting algorithm where the smallest or largest element is selected from the entire sequence and swapped with the first element, then the next smallest or largest is selected and swapped with the second element, and so on.

66. SQL Query: An SQL query is a statement used to extract data from a database. SQL queries are used to query the database to retrieve, update, or delete data in a specific way. SQL queries can include operations such as selecting specific columns from a table, applying filters to retrieve only desired data, sorting results, and aggregating data.

SQL queries are written using the Structured Query Language (SQL), which is a query language used to communicate with relational databases.

# Index

1. Introduction pg.4

2. Installing SQLite pg.8

3. Creating and Managing SQLite Tables pg.12

4. Creating a Table pg.17

5. Definition of table fields pg.21

6. Modifying the table structure pg.25

7. Deleting a SQLite table pg.30

8. SQLite CRUD Operations pg.33

9. Data Insertion and Data Reading pg.38

10. Updating Data and Deleting Data in SQLite pg.43

11. Using SQL commands to create queries pg.47

12.Using SQLite built-in functions pg.50

13.Using subquery and JOIN operations pg.53

14.Introduction to transactions and transaction execution in SQLite pg.57

15.Commit and rollback of transactions in SQLite pg.60

16.Transaction Management in case of error in SQLite pg.63

17.Database Backup Database Restore from a Backup pg.67

18.Backup Creation Backup File Management in SQLite pg.70

19.Using Indexes to Improve Performance in SQLite pg.74

20.Using cache to optimize queries Query Optimization in SQLite pg.78

21.Security pg.83

**22.Error handling pg.87**

**23.Practical Examples in SQLite pg.91**

**24.Basic Glossary pg.96**

www.ingramcontent.com/pod-product-compliance
Lightning Source LLC
Chambersburg PA
CBHW071521220526
45472CB00003B/1111